A GENTLE VOICE IS
CALLING YOUR HEART....

He calls Himself
"the Good Shepherd,"
but what does that mean?
Is it just a pleasant metaphor,
a gentle parable?
Or could it be something
far greater
that could influence your life
for all eternity?

The Little Books of Why™

WHY A SHEPHERD?

Bodie & Brock Thoene

PARABLE
SAN LUIS OBISPO, CALIFORNIA
OUTREACH
VISTA, CALIFORNIA

The Little Books of Why™ by Bodie and Brock Thoene are produced by Parable, 3563 Empleo Street, San Luis Obispo, CA 93401 and Outreach, Inc., 2230 Oak Ridge Way, Vista, CA 92081. Visit parable.com or outreach.com.

Printed in the United States of America
12 11 10 09 08 07
7 6 5 4 3 2

CONTENTS

INTRODUCTION

SHEPHERDS CAMP

Central California, 1959

Bodie Thoene

It was 1959, the hottest summer on record.

I was eight years old when I first attended Shepherds Camp in the mountains above Central California. The experience remains among my most wonderful childhood memories.

Our teacher at Shepherds Camp was a real-life shepherdess named Maria. She was Basque—a widow in her early forties who came from the Spanish Pyrenees mountains. The rumor among the women in our neighborhood was that Maria had lost her husband and three small children in the Spanish Civil War, during the Nazi bombing of Madrid. It was one of those real-life tragedies that made my mother's friends shake their heads and say in hushed voices, "Oh, kid! Poor thing. How does she go on living?"

But even after such a loss, Maria did go on with life. Destitute after World War II, she and her father, old Papa Raul, immigrated to Central California to tend the sheep of a wealthy Basque relative, whom they called "the *patrone*."

I remember her as a tall, cheerful woman with hips much broader than her shoulders. Salt-and-pepper hair was thick, curly, and cropped short above her ears. It was the same length all over and had the consistency of a black lamb's fleece. (I learned later that she and Papa Raul took turns cutting one another's hair with sheep shears.)

Papa Raul wore a battered straw cowboy hat, so his identical haircut was only visible when he removed his hat indoors. He was still strong and straight, though he was in his seventies when I first knew him. His skin was the same consistency as his weathered leather boots. He was slim-hipped but had a big belly that almost concealed his prized silver-belt buckle, won in the sheep-shearing contest at the annual Wool Growers' picnic.

Maria and Papa Raul were ever-present personalities in our little world. I remember her expansive laugh and enormous smiles for all the little children as she dished up barbeque at the church bazaars at Christ the King. We often saw Maria and Papa Raul at Wool Growers' Restaurant, where she waited on tables and where we ate with friends and family at least once a week.

Maria spoke passable English and at least

three other Latin-based languages. Old Papa
Raul, on the other hand, seemed to understand only the Basque language. There was a
black eye patch over his left eye, and a deep
scar stitched down his cheek—the result of
an encounter with a young mountain lion
stealing a lamb from the flock. Even disfig-
ured, his face conveyed a remarkable variety
of expressions as Maria translated the con-
versation of others from English into Basque
and back again. He would smile and nod, and
nod again as she spoke for him.

She seemed especially fond of me, clasp-
ing my face in her rough hands and kissing
me on the top of my head at every greeting.
"Oh, you little Bo! You big brown eyes. You
red curls. Oh! I teach you Basque so you understand when old Papa can tell you himself
how sweet."

I overheard my aunt Margaret say that,
with brown eyes and red hair at age eight, I
closely resembled the oldest of Maria's little
daughters killed in the war. "Oh, kid! How

does she bear it?" Aunt Margaret would murmur.

Shepherds Camp 1959 leapt into being one May evening at Wool Growers' Restaurant. My mother and the five women who were her best friends, all working women, discussed what to do with the kids once school was out: Girl Scout Camp? Dude ranch for another? A trip to Grandmother's house in Stockton? A long-term babysitter? It all sounded pretty boring.

At that very moment Maria emerged from the kitchen with a huge bowl of Basque soup and a basket of bread for our long table. She looked at me, then addressed my mother. "Better they learn to work than sit around bored in Bakersfield heat. Papa and me take the *patrone's* flock up to Tobias meadows this summer. Let the kids come up to the tablelands with me and Papa Raul. We teach 'em how to be good shepherds. Like David in the Bible, yes? You know the story of King David tending his sheep, yes? To be a good shepherd means something."

My mother's friends looked at one another as though Maria had fallen from heaven and spoken with the voice of an angel. The Twenty-third Psalm suddenly became the creed for summer camp! Green pastures. Still waters. Fresh air. Camping under the stars. Responsibility. Learning to care for woolly little lambs. What could be more idyllic?

"What do you think, Little Bo? You want to be a shepherd?" my mother asked.

From that evening on, we counted the days and hours until school was out and we could join Maria and Papa Raul for an adventure in the Tobias meadows. Little could we imagine then what *good shepherd* meant…or how much of an influence it would have over our lives.

Why a shepherd? Maria was right. It means something. It really means something.

WHY A SHEPHERD?

*What kind of shepherd
do you want to follow?*

Savior, like a shepherd lead us,
much we need Thy tender care;
In Thy pleasant pastures feed us,
for our use Thy folds prepare.
Blessed Jesus, blessed Jesus!
Thou hast bought us, Thine we are.
Blessed Jesus, blessed Jesus!
Thou hast bought us, Thine we are.

—"SAVIOR, LIKE A SHEPHERD LEAD US"
VERSE 1, WORDS BY DOROTHY A. THRUPP, 1836

SEEKING THE GOOD SHEPHERD

When you think of the Good Shepherd, what images come to your mind? The Gospel writers recorded dozens of descriptive phrases that Jesus used to describe Himself. In the Gospel of John alone we find: Son of Man (John 1:51; 3:13); Bread of Life (John 6:35); Light of the World (John 8:12; 9:5); The Way, the Truth, and the Life (John 14:6). Perhaps the most often quoted is the title Jesus claimed in John 3:16 and elsewhere: The Son of God.

Each of these terms or phrases carries an important message about who Jesus is, about His mission, His message, and how we are to regard our relationship with Him in the scope of eternity.

But in *Why a Shepherd?* we'll focus on how Jesus described Himself in John 10: The Good Shepherd.

I am the Good Shepherd. The Good Shepherd risks and lays down His own life for the sheep. But the hired servant (he who merely serves for wages) who is neither the shepherd nor the owner of the sheep, when he sees the wolf coming, deserts the flock and runs away. And the wolf chases and snatches them and scatters the flock. Now the hireling flees because he merely serves for wages and is not himself concerned about the sheep (cares nothing for them). I am the Good Shepherd; and I know and recognize My own, and My own know and recognize Me—Even as truly as the Father knows Me and I also know the Father—and I am giving My very own life and laying it down on behalf of the sheep. And I have other sheep beside these who are not of this fold. I must bring and impel those also; and they will listen to My voice and heed my call, and so there will be (they will become) one flock under one Shepherd.

—JOHN 10:11-16, AMP

Of all the comparisons Jesus applied to Himself, He spent the most concentrated amount of time—as recorded by the apostle John—in making certain His listeners understood what He meant when He said, "I am the Good Shepherd."

Why is it important for Jesus to describe Himself this way? And why does He define the Good Shepherd as one who is willing to die for the flock under his care? Who is the "hireling" or the faithless shepherd? And, for that matter, who are the sheep?

The secrets are waiting to be revealed....

WHY A SHEPHERD'S HEART?

To a shepherd,
it's not just a job.
It's a way of life.

The King of love my Shepherd is,
Whose goodness faileth never,
I nothing lack if I am His
And He is mine forever.

—"THE KING OF LOVE MY SHEPHERD IS"
VERSE 1, WORDS BY HENRY W. BAKER, 1868

GREEN PASTURES
AND STILL WATERS...

There were only four girls and four boys, all
ages eight to ten, who would spend the summer learning to tend the flocks. Older and
younger brothers and sisters were consigned
to North of the River day-camp programs
in the heat of the Central Valley. Maria and
Papa Raul wisely decided that ages eight to
ten were the perfect ages to learn. We were
old enough to work and take instruction, but
not yet old enough to have reached the surly
wilderness called adolescence.

"Eight to ten," Maria explained. "Tender
hearts. These have shepherds' hearts; eager
hearts that will listen and hear and follow the
voice of the chief shepherd."

For the last few weeks of third grade, we
chosen few hung out together on the play-
ground, talking of green pastures and still
waters.

Doc Batista, the local veterinarian and my

parents' dear friend, taught me all about parasites in large animals. I memorized the names of worms. For science class I was allowed to take to school formaldehyde bottles of sheep parasites as seen in their various stages of development. I brought the display home after my presentation and set them up in a colorful row on the shelf next to my dolls. My life was transformed. I made the declaration over dinner that I wanted to be a vet like Doc and deliver sheep from evil parasites.

Mama's enthusiasm waxed very thin, and the bottles of sheep worms were returned to Doc's office with an effusive but conclusive thank-you note.

Mama encouraged me to concentrate more on the pastoral, Little Bo Peep aspect of my upcoming adventure. A list of approved gear included three pair of Levis, three long-sleeved, snap-button shirts, cowboy boots, sneakers, thick socks and underwear for a week, a jacket, bathing suit, shorts, wide-brimmed straw cowboy hat, sleeping bag, and a fishing pole.

My father, showing me how to pack everything neatly into my duffel bag, said he wished he were eight years old again.

Mama fussed about the potential of insect stings, sunburns, and staying warm and dry.

Each night at bedtime Mama taught me to recite the Twenty-third Psalm by heart. Hardly able to sleep with excitement, I counted sheep at bedtime and dreamed of the moment of departure: *"The Lord is my shepherd, I shall not want..."*

I learned the words, yet could not comprehend the depth of the psalm's meaning. Only real-life experience living among the sheep and shepherds in the high country could bring true insight. Those who lived in the Israel of King David and heard the psalms of the shepherd-king would have understood perfectly the power of the lyrics...and the broad-reaching scope and importance of the job.

WHY STAND WATCH?

Danger can come from the most
innocent-looking of places...
and bring death
to an unwitting sheep.

When I walk through the shades of death,
Thy presence is my stay;
one word of Thy supporting breath
drives all my fears away.

—"MY SHEPHERD WILL SUPPLY MY NEED"
VERSE 3, WORDS BY ISAAC WATTS (1674-1748)

A SURPRISING SEARCH

My parents drove all morning up the narrow road into the mountains. We rendezvoused with the other kids and Maria at the camp in a high mountain meadow.

Tents were erected near a beat-up little camp trailer. A kettle of soup simmered over an open fire. I could smell bread baking in a Dutch oven buried in the coals. The pasture glistened green and lush and empty beside a creek.

"Where are the lambs?" I asked.

"You will meet them soon enough," Maria replied, signaling two black-and-white border collies to stand in the line with us for inspection of hands before lunch. "But first we must prepare the table for them."

We shared a wonderful meal of Basque soup and bread that seemed better than any I had ever tasted, even at the Wool Growers' Restaurant.

"The Lord is my shepherd. I shall not want."

It was just after noon when my father hugged me good-bye and told me to DO good. Mama hugged me and told me to BE good. Both were very important instructions for a Junior Shepherd, I was to learn. I brushed back a tear and resisted the temptation to turn and run after my folks as they drove away.

Maria gave each of us navy blue berets, like the kind we had seen on the Basque sheepherders.

"But where ARE the lambs?" my best friend, Simona, asked.

Maria waved a hand toward the empty meadow. "They will arrive in three days with Papa Raul. But first it is our job to prepare the tableland for them. Just as I had a wonderful meal ready for you when you came, yes? We must get the meal ready for the flock. This pasture seems very beautiful if you are a sheep, yes? But the good shepherd searches for danger and knows it is also still very dangerous."

"Dangerous?" We were all surprised by

her serious expression.

"Yes." She produced a plant from a cardboard box. Its roots were still intact in a ball of soil.

"This is the first enemy of the flock. 'Locoweed,' the old ones call it. Hidden in the lovely green grass are these poisonous plants that every good shepherd knows must be dug out...completely taken out...by the roots. To leave even a little behind will cost the life of one of our precious little ones. Or the ewes will eat it and nothing else. They will starve and grow very sick and perhaps die. When they fall, they cannot stand again. They become prey for other creatures. Locoweed is very bad."

Maria clucked her tongue. "So we shepherds are here before our lambs to search every inch of the meadow and clear out the locoweed before they are allowed to enter."

Maria showed us the noxious plant and instructed us on the proper procedure for removal. Locoweed had to be removed by the roots, dug up, heaped up and burned, before the flock came anywhere near the tableland. One leaf left untended, one root remaining in the rich soil, could result in a violent and painful death for a grazing lamb. The enemy of a beloved lamb, it seemed, was not always something as fierce as a bear or a wolf or a mountain lion, but something as harmless in appearance as a thin, white, trumpet-shaped flower blooming in a broad-leafed plant.

Camouflaged within the richness of the Tobias pasturage, the deadly plant seemed at first invisible to our eyes. But it was there. For the next three days we walked a careful grid pattern across the meadow, searching for clumps of locoweed.

East to west. West to east. South to north. North to south.

The boys dug out the plants. Our little fingers combed the soil, searching for any remaining roots that might sprout overnight and provide temptation and death for our lambs. We soon learned to recognize the weed, and we pounced on it with fierce enthusiasm.

There was so much of it!

A bonfire, heaped high with locoweed, was the end result of our quest.

"You prepare a table before me" (Psalm 23:5).

Ever since those first days at Shepherds Camp I have never heard the words of the Shepherd's Psalm without remembering how Jesus our Shepherd searches our lives for sin, like blossoming locoweed. As the sharp eyes of the Holy Spirit comb the deep soil of our hearts in search of bitter roots that might sprout and somehow poison our lives and the lives of those around us, what might be revealed?

When one ailing sheep lags behind the others
And loses itself in the sylvan mazes,
Tearing its white fleece on the thorns and briars,
Sharp in the brambles,
Unwearied the Shepherd, that lost one seeking,
Drives away the wolves and on His strong shoulders
Brings it home again to the fold's safekeeping,
Healed and unsullied.

He brings it back to the green fields and meadows,
Where no thorn bush waves with its cruel prickles,
Where no shaggy thistle arms trembling branches
With its tough briars.

But where palm trees grow in the open woodland,
Where the lush grass bends its
green leaves, and laurels
Shade the glassy streamlet of living water
Ceaselessly flowing.

—"THE SHEEP RESTORED TO VERDANT FIELDS"
PRUDENTIUS (348-410 A.D.)
FROM POEMS OF PRUDENTIUS
TRANSLATED BY SR. M. CLEMENT EAGAN

THE PARABLE OF THE LOST SHEEP

Jesus told them this parable: Suppose one of you has a hundred sheep and loses one of them. Does he not leave the ninety-nine in the open country and go after the lost sheep until he finds it? And when he finds it, he joyfully puts it on his shoulders and goes home. Then he calls his friends and neighbors together and says, "Rejoice with me; I have found my lost sheep." I tell you that in the same way there will be more rejoicing in heaven over one sinner who repents than over ninety-nine righteous persons who do not need to repent.

—LUKE 15:3-7

A LIFE LESSON

Why would a shepherd seek a stubborn sheep? Why not give up? Let the sheep go its own way? Get its just due?

Perhaps the best explanation of all is from Zadok, the feisty, first-century shepherd in our novel *Sixth Covenant*, as he talks with Yosef of Nazareth.

Zadok stood on the knoll overlooking the vast
sea of woolly sheep that moved slowly down
the ravine. He clutched his new staff in his left
hand. His rod, a blunt stick about the length of
a man's forearm, hung from a leather strap on
his right wrist.

A young ewe spotted green grass beside a
steep drop-off. She left the trail. Zadok whistled
for her to turn. When she did not heed his voice,
he flung the rod with perfect aim to skim her
nose. Startled by the rod, she scampered back
among her fellows.

"She's a stubborn one, that one is." Zadok
motioned for his dog to fetch back the throwing
stick. "She'll go her own way nine times out of
ten." He glanced at the crook of the staff. "That's
the purpose of the hook on a staff. It'll see some
hard use pullin' her up when she falls. Gettin'
her out of tight places. A fine gift, Yosef."

Yosef kept his eye riveted on the errant ewe
who, even though she came back into line, was

still searching for a blade of grass to claim as her own. "I never thought of them as having their own minds."

Zadok laughed. "Just like humankind, they are! No different at all. It's no mistake the Lord has called us his sheep. Stubborn, stupid, timid, foolish, careless, greedy. Prone t' follow wherever the flock goes...even over a cliff if others was runnin' that way. And yet some'll find a way t' escape the lush green pastures we lead them to. Aye. Out of pure cussedness they'll run after a blade of grass on a desolate mountainside. The Eternal has used these dumb, stubborn sheep—of all animals on earth—t' teach us how much he loves his people Israel. That's why we carry the rod and staff. I can throw so as t' turn back a wolf from devourin' a lamb. Or I can use the rod t' correct and turn back a sheep who is goin' away from my protection. When I strike, it hurts the sheep. Aye. But at least she's alive."

Zadok waved the rod aloft. "Maybe that ewe will figure out one day that I do what I do for her good and the good of all. If not, one day she'll slip away out of range of my rod and staff. And she'll be pulled down and killed by a jackal who lies in wait. I will have done all I could. Some sheep refuse my protection. Some will not be saved. Aye. There's lessons a'plenty in the sheep."

—Sixth Covenant

WHY WORRY?

It's the little things—
the maddening distractions—
that interrupt a sheep's rest.

He makes me lie down in green pastures.
He leads me beside still waters.
He restores my soul.

—Psalm 23:2-3, ESV

THE WORRIES

"We call them The Worries," Maria instructed as we observed the swarms of flies that arrived at the meadow with the sheep.

My father had told me to DO good. So I fulfilled part of that promise every day by dressing the sensitive heads, ears, noses, and eyes of my lambs with a special ointment meant to protect them from pesky insects.

"You anoint my head with oil" (Psalm 23:5).

Who could have imagined that the greatest enemies of a sheep are actually the smallest creatures on the mountain? But it's true. Flies, ticks, mosquitoes—insects of all kinds—swarmed around our sheep like a cloud of worries. It was our job to protect them from the anxiety of those maddening distractions and discouragements.

I knew about parasites from my science project. My display had included a sample of larvae from botflies, which lay their eggs in the soft tissue around the face of an animal.

But a sample in a jar had not prepared me for the fierceness of these pests. As if the buzzing of flies was not enough to drive the sheep mad, some larvae were ingested through their food supply and then hatched in their digestive system, robbing the sheep of nutrients. No matter how well-fed a sheep was, if it was troubled by flies or infested with parasites, it grew thin and weak, unable to eat, and never achieved the full potential of its growth.

The first day the flock arrived in our clean, lush pasture devoid of locoweed, we knew that the sheep had brought the insects with them, polluting the peace of the landscape. The ewes and their babies were restless, unhappy, and irritable with one another beneath the barrage of buzzing flies.

Papa Raul scratched his bristly face and opened a can of balm. He held up his hand and waded into the flock, proving to us just how little it took for a good shepherd to soothe the torment of worries for his ewes and lambs.

Maria translated instructions to the rest of us as he dabbed a little ointment onto the most sensitive skin and spread a thin layer of protection. Then we proceeded to apply the balm to our own lambs.

The gentle oil on the heads, faces, and undersides of our ewes and lambs offered a first line of defense against the worrying irritation of insects that seemed to follow the flocks no matter where they were pastured.

I was amazed. The first drops of warm oil applied around the eyes and nose had the power to suddenly transform a nervous, fretting creature into a calm and docile personality.

"Sheep are a lot like people." Maria smiled. "It's little things that disturb their rest. So the sheep depend on us to protect them from these small things. If they run from us, we cannot cover them. But you see? Look how they come to Papa Raul and put their heads in his hands! See? They trust he will take care of them."

When I hear the words "*You anoint my head with oil*" (Psalm 23:5), I remember how the sheep hurried to place their heads into the hands of the good shepherd for protection.

It was because they trusted him to be their guardian...and because the shepherd knew exactly what tools to use.

We are Thine, Thou dost befriend us,
be the guardian of our way;
Keep Thy flock, from sin defend us,
seek us when we go astray.
Blessed Jesus, blessed Jesus!
Hear, O hear us when we pray.
Blessed Jesus, blessed Jesus!
Hear, O hear us when we pray.

—"SAVIOR, LIKE A SHEPHERD LEAD US"
VERSE 2, WORDS BY DOROTHY A. THRUPP, 1836

WHY AN ENEMY?

Someone is after you…
and he's serious.

Be self-controlled and alert.
Your enemy the devil
prowls around
like a roaring lion
looking for someone
to devour.
Resist him, standing firm.

—1 PETER 5:8-9

THE SAME FOR OVER 2000 YEARS...

The sheep that lived when Jesus walked the earth and the sheep of today are threatened by the same enemies.

There are the obvious predators: lions, bears, wolves, leopards, jackals, hyenas, and thieves. Where we raised our family's sheep and lambs, they were threatened by mountain lions and coyotes.

Then there are the insidious dangers: bad water, poisonous plants, such as the locoweed we searched for at Shepherds Camp, venomous snakes, and the realities of getting lost and falling into difficulty without the shepherd around to help.

But there is an even more obvious predator who is out to get the sheep. And he's tenaciously interested in a different kind of sheep—the human sheep God loves.

Sheep like you.

RESISTING THE LION

The Bible portrays Satan as "*a roaring lion, looking for someone to devour.*" But here's the good news Satan doesn't want you to know: he is already defeated!

"*Resist the devil,*" we are told, "*and he will flee from you*" (James 4:7, ESV). It is the power of Jesus' name that gives us the ability to resist. Because Satan wants to attack and tear down those who believe in Jesus, he will always be looking for ways to interfere with your relationship with the Lord; to draw you away from your faith and trust in God. But recognizing these attempts and drawing on the power of Jesus' name is the same as having the Good Shepherd standing between you and harm, brandishing His staff.

First Peter 5:6-7 says: "*Humble yourselves, therefore, under the mighty hand of God… casting all your anxieties on Him, because He cares for you.*"

No lion, no wolf, no evil can harm you

while you remain close to the Good Shepherd…while you are within the circle of his care. It's only when we wander away—when we decide to be obstinate and self-willed, giving in to the promptings of ego or envy—that we take ourselves outside the protection of the Good Shepherd.

And make no mistake. Outside a close, personal relationship with the Master, there *are* lions and wolves waiting to devour you. If you go beyond what you know to be right, the moment you flirt with sin you put space between yourself and the Shepherd. It's not that He is powerless to save you even then, or that He will say, "What's one sheep more or less? If that one wants to wander off, then let him." Oh, no! He'll never say that. Remember why the shepherd would leave the ninety-nine sheep and head off to find the one? But what needless pain and sorrow you will endure until you call out to Him for help!

When you put yourself needlessly in harm's way, you create difficulty for yourself.

Like the sheep that wanders far away, you can put a hill—a hill you can't see over—between you and the safety zone of your home.

THE DISGUISED DANGERS...

There are also subtle things that threaten you: feeding away from safe pasture...indulging in things that will poison your soul. Things that may appear innocent or harmless are like locoweed to a flock of sheep.

Gulping large swallows of anxiety, wallowing in self-pity, devouring gossip—these are all self-destructive behaviors that poison the soul. But all can be avoided by staying close to the side of the Shepherd.

Thy hand, in sight of all my foes,
  Doth still my table spread;
My cup with blessings overflows,
  Thy oil anoints my head.

The sure provisions of my God
  Attend me all my days;
Oh, may Thy house be mine abode
  And all my work be praise.

There would I find a settled rest,
  While others go and come;
No more a stranger or a guest,
  But like a child at home.

—"MY SHEPHERD WILL SUPPLY MY NEED"
VERSES 4-6, WORDS BY ISAAC WATTS (1674-1748)

WHY A ROD AND A STAFF?

*Of all the tools
a shepherd could use,
why these?*

In death's dark vale I fear no ill
With Thee, dear Lord, beside me;
Thy rod and staff my comfort still,
Thy cross before to guide me.

—"THE KING OF LOVE MY SHEPHERD IS"
VERSE 4, WORDS BY HENRY W. BAKER, 1868

STARGAZING

My first real memory of stars was looking into the night sky from the high mountain meadow where the flock slept beneath the watchful gaze of Papa Raul. Hour by hour, lantern in hand, the old man and his favorite sheepdog slowly walked around the perimeter of the pasture.

Unlike the shepherd-king David, who had carried a stout staff and a sling, Papa Raul shouldered a World War II surplus M-1 carbine as he made his rounds. The beam of his lamp bobbed through the darkness, marking his progress and warning any night predators that he was on duty.

Like the flock of sheep, we children also lay under the stars, warm and secure in our sleeping bags.

"There is the Lion." Maria drew our attention heavenward as she pointed out the sickle-shaped formation of stars that made the lion's mane. I could see the head clearly as I followed the sweep of her hand. "You see him? The stars are pictures of Christ. Like in a church window, yes? Only God put the pictures in the stars for us shepherds who can't go to church because we must watch the sheep."

I pointed to one of the formations. "What is that? It looks like a teapot."

"That's the Archer. He draws his bow. When I see him, I think of King David's friend, Jonathan, who shot the arrow as a warning to David. But I also think he looks like a teapot, no? And that is the Milky Way spouting from the teapot. So many stars pouring out. God is pouring tea for the angels."

Thus proceeded Maria's imaginative bedtime stories. Right there in Tobias meadows, we learned life-transforming lessons on the true identity of Christ as declared in the constellations and in the Bible. Her parables combined the watchfulness of shepherds and the loving God who pours tea for His angels. What child wouldn't have been captivated?

"He makes me lie down in green pastures….I will fear no evil, for You are with me; Your rod and your staff, they comfort me" (Psalm 23:2, 4, ESV).

When I first learned the wonderful words of David's psalm about the Good Shepherd, I did not know that in real life, sheep slept standing up…ever ready to run and scatter at the first sign of danger. Unless sheep felt completely secure and protected, they would not lie down, no matter how green the pastures or still the waters.

Papa Raul did not sleep after dark—not ever. He alone remained watchful and ready to meet any threat as he scanned the darkness for the yellow glint of a predator's eyes. The hiss of his old Coleman lantern was like a lullaby as he circled us in constant vigil.

All the sheep and the kids of Papa Raul's flock lay down in the green pasture and slept without fear through the night. Why? Because they knew the shepherd was ever watchful. His presence was their comfort. His rod and staff were their protection.

TOOLS OF THE TRADE

Curiously, only two tools are mentioned in the Bible in connection with keeping watch over a flock of sheep: a rod and a staff. In today's world a shepherd's equipment may include pickup trucks and high-powered rifles. In some places shepherds may even use airplanes. But with most flocks in less-developed nations, shepherds still operate with only these same two basic implements.

Strange, isn't it, that these tools haven't changed in thousands of years? They are the same tools that ancient shepherds used when they first domesticated and reared sheep.

But what are a *rod* and a *staff*?

Though they may sound similar in English, *rod* and *staff* are not synonyms.

The rod
The rod is a short, stout stick. If you think of a cudgel, you'd be close to the truth. It has

two purposes: defense and discipline. Where rods are still in everyday use, shepherds can wield them not only as clubs but also fling them with great accuracy. A skulking coyote can be driven off by a well-placed throw of a rod. Even a lion attempting to snatch a lamb will beat a hasty retreat if clubbed on the head with a hickory branch wielded with a shepherd's full strength.

The rod also represents an extension of the shepherd's control over his flock. If an obstinate sheep is heading into trouble or sneaking away from the safety of the flock, a flip of the rod into the offender's face will turn the wanderer around. Besides being embarrassing to the sheep (who wants to get corrected in front of your peers?), such correction may cause pain.

We may think the shepherd was too rough, too harsh with his correction. But such thoughts only exist because we are built closer to the earth. From the vantage point the shepherd has, he can see much farther.

He can spot the rattlesnake hiding in the innocent-seeming clump of brush. He can see over the rock pile to where the lion is waiting. He recognizes the lethal plants growing amid the inviting foliage.

The Hebrew word translated *rod* is *shebet*. Besides carrying the meaning "stick" or "club," it also is sometimes translated "scepter," carrying again the notion of a king's authority. Interestingly, *shebet* also relates to "tribe," "clan," or "family." This is a reminder that God expects families to have discipline and instruction. It also means God frequently uses circumstances involving our families to teach us lessons…especially ones about patience and the setting aside of pride!

The staff

The other implement universal to shepherds the world over is the staff. This longer stick, often with a crook at the end that is unique to sheep rearing, represents a shepherd's protection and his ability to rescue his flock from harm. During his long tramps through the fields with his sheep, a shepherd relies on his staff as a walking stick. Over the night watches the shepherd often leans on his staff. In other words, where the shepherd's staff is located, there the shepherd himself will always be found. That means if a sheep rests near the shepherd's staff, no harm can possibly befall that sheep.

A staff can discourage a charging bear or smash the head of a snake. The crook is used to gently lift a wayward lamb back to its mother's side, or to free a sheep trapped amid the thorns.

The staff is the extension of the shepherd's authority. It says that even if a sheep has wandered so far as to get into danger, that sheep still belongs to the shepherd. And the shepherd will rescue it.

But what do the rod and the staff have to do with you?

SOMETHING TO PONDER...

If the Lord Himself is our Good Shepherd, as He claims throughout the Bible, He is the master of the rod and staff. He wields His power to protect us from harm.

And what good news! There is no evil we face that He cannot defeat, no danger He cannot overcome.

When He turns you back from harm, even by painful discipline, it is for your well-being, to keep you safe. When He won't let you have something you thought you couldn't live without, when He prevents you from going where your heart longed to go—it is only because He can see farther and clearer than you.

He, the Good Shepherd, is ever watchful over you.

Thou hast promised to receive us,
poor and sinful though we be;
Thou hast mercy to relieve us,
grace to cleanse and power to free.
Blessed Jesus, blessed Jesus!
We will early turn to Thee.
Blessed Jesus, blessed Jesus!
We will early turn to Thee.

—"SAVIOR, LIKE A SHEPHERD LEAD US"
VERSE 3, WORDS BY DOROTHY A. THRUPP, 1836

WHY THESE SHEPHERDS?

*Jesus is the culmination
of a long line
of model shepherds.*

My shepherd will supply my need,
Jehovah is His name;
In pastures fresh He makes me feed
Beside the living stream.
He brings my wandering spirit back
When I forsake His ways,
And leads me, for His mercy's sake,
In paths of truth and grace.

—"My Shepherd Will Supply My Need"
verses 1-2, words by Isaac Watts (1675-1748)

A LIFE OF HAZARDS

Among the patriarchs of ancient Israel were many shepherds and herdsmen. In fact Abraham, Isaac, Jacob, Joseph, Moses, and David were all shepherds or flock owners. Some, like David, rose from obscurity as shepherds to be fathers of nations or kings. Others, like Moses, left behind wealth and privilege as God put him through rigorous training and discipline before using him as a shepherd of His people.

Psalm 23's picture seems very pastoral and peaceful: *"He makes me lie down in green pastures. He leads me beside still waters"* (verses 1-2, ESV). Except for one problem. That picture applies to the sheep—not necessarily to the life of the shepherd!

If we stop and consider what Jesus said about how the shepherd must protect the sheep from wolves, then we acknowledge that a shepherd's life is not without hazards. Yet even then we expect those hazards to be from wild animals and from other hardships of living out in the open.

But such would not seem to be the case when we consider the fates of other noteworthy shepherds recorded in Scripture.

Abel

The second-born son of Adam and Eve, Abel is also the first shepherd mentioned specifically in the Bible. In obedience to God's command, he offered the firstborn male lamb from his flock as a sacrifice to God. His brother, Cain, chose instead to approach God on his own terms, rather than according to God's will. Abel's sacrifice was approved; Cain's was not. As a result, Cain hated his brother enough to kill him.

So the story of the first shepherd is also linked with the unreasoning hatred and jealousy of a brother, the setting of Cain's will in opposition to God's, and the first death recorded in Scripture...a *murder* at that. The first shepherd—an obedient man, approved by God—was killed by his own brother. Instead of accepting the rebuke of self-will and seeing in Abel's success an example to be followed, Cain took his brother's life…just as Jesus' kinsmen would demand Jesus' life in order to silence Him several thousand years later.

Joseph

The story of Joseph's coat of many colors is another tale of persecution because of envy. Joseph's older brothers hated him because they perceived that their father, Jacob, favored him. Because of Joseph's prophetic dreams, his brothers also called him proud and accused him of wanting to "lord it over them."

As a result, when his own brothers were tending the sheep, they sold him into slavery. Jacob's grief nearly killed him when his own sons lied to him about how Joseph had been killed by a wild animal.

In Egypt Joseph was falsely accused and

thrown into prison. He languished there a long time before God used the power of Joseph's dream interpretation to advance him to the second highest position in the land... just in time to rescue his entire family, father and brothers, from a terrible famine.

Moses

Though not raised in a family of sheepherders, Moses took up this occupation when he fled from Egypt. While Moses was tending sheep, God met him in the burning bush, then sent him back to Egypt to be His representative before Pharaoh. There Moses exchanged the shepherding of a flock of sheep for the leading of an entire nation of Israelites. He constantly faced grumbling and rejection and envy, but through it all his emblem of authority and the mark of God's power in his life remained the staff of a shepherd. It was that staff he would raise over the waters of the Red Sea.

The parting of the Red Sea is a good

reminder for all of us: never confuse mere facts with truth! The fact was that Israel was trapped between the sea and the murderous Egyptian army. The greater Truth is that God is perfectly capable of parting the sea with the staff of a shepherd, leading His people to safety, and utterly destroying the enemies who try and follow. Ponder that the next time you think of a simple shepherd's staff!

David

Before he was the powerful king of Israel, David was a shepherd. In fact, when David volunteered to fight Goliath, he cited his experience as a shepherd in defending the sheep from lions and bears. He said God had enabled him to pursue marauding wild animals with his staff and his slingshot as he rescued his father's sheep from their clutches, so why would he be afraid of a braggart giant?

As the youngest of eight brothers, David was the one left out with the sheep when the prophet Samuel arrived at David's father's house. Yet Samuel chose to pass over all seven elder brothers and anointed David to be king of Israel. This choice didn't set well with the other brothers. Later, just before the battle with Goliath, David's eldest brother made fun of him for being merely a shepherd, then turned around and derided David for abandoning his duties to "come see the battle."

The shepherds at Bethlehem
As we wrote in our novel *Sixth Covenant*, the awe and wonder of the night of Jesus' birth would be forever entrenched in the minds and hearts of the shepherds of Bethlehem....

Tonight everything had seemed so ordinary: A young woman in labor urgently seeking shelter in a village packed with travelers. A baby boy born in the warmth of Bethlehem's lambing cave. It was hard to see the miracle in that.

Yet it was a miracle. The Son of God reached out to the world from the womb of a virgin as the prophets foretold. The first bleating cry of His voice was heard from the midst of firstborn male lambs destined for Temple sacrifice. Perhaps one day it would all make sense, but tonight the meaning remained a puzzle to the participants in the drama.

The brilliant transitory star that shone as first herald of the birth of the true King of Israel faded and vanished. The sign of two bright planets, which had been dancing within the constellation of Israel for months, was now concealed behind a layer of clouds that closed in over the territory of Ephratha.

The chill of a coming snowstorm was in the

air. Shepherds stamped their feet and stretched out hands to the watch fires in an effort to stay warm. The rhythm of life in Bethlehem resumed. There were things to do. Tasks to accomplish.

After the birth, Rachel, midwife of Bethlehem who tended Mary and her child, had called for more water to be drawn from the ancient well of David. It had been heated to bathe the Son of David. But Rachel had not considered God's covenant with King David as she'd washed the film of Mary's blood from the newborn's ruddy skin. The baby had simply been in need of washing, like all newborn babies.

Those shepherds who had seen and heard the angels from the pastures of Migdal Eder scanned the skies and hoped for more heavenly proclamations to resound from the hills of the terraced amphitheater of Bethlehem. Had anyone ever witnessed such glory before this night? What could it mean?

But instead of angel voices, the soft song of the infant's young mother drifted out to a dozen rough shepherds. "Hush, my babe, lie still and slumber...."

So young, Mary was. Why was she chosen by Yahweh to give birth to the one the angels called Immanu'el, "God-with-us"? Could it be?

It had not happened in the way anyone had imagined it. Mary of Nazareth. Betrothed wife of Yosef of Nazareth. Not much more than a girl and so...ordinary. Yet the angels had declared that this was the birth of the Son of David! This baby boy was the fulfillment of every prophecy in Torah. The hope of all generations in Israel!

—*Sixth Covenant*

The shepherds of Bethlehem, first witnesses to the arrival of the Messiah, were privileged to hear the heavenly choir. But they also lost their own sons to Herod's murderous rage.

The lot of a shepherd has never been an easy one. When Jesus said, "*A good shepherd lays down his life for the sheep*" (John 10:11), it was not merely because the sheep were threatened by wild animals. Human wolves also waited to attack. The pattern of our Good Shepherd Jesus' condemnation and execution was written throughout Scripture for all to see.

WHY THE DIFFERENCE?

*How can you tell the difference
between a faithful shepherd
and a faithless shepherd?*

"There's a rule among us. It's written in here."
Zadok tapped his chest. "A good shepherd'll
lay down his life for the safety of the flock.
Are there those in charge of sheep who don't care?
Aye. There are hired men who'll turn tail at the
first sign of danger. They let their master's sheep die
and never think twice about it. But we men of Bethlehem...
we're hereditary shepherds of the Lord's own flocks.
We walk the path David walked. Our shepherd-king."

—Sixth Covenant

WHO ARE FALSE SHEPHERDS?

Many of us are familiar with the description Jesus applied to Himself as "the Good Shepherd." We understand that a good shepherd is fearless, standing up almost bare-handed against bears and lions and wolves that threaten the sheep. We readily comprehend that a Good Shepherd is even willing to sacrifice his own life to protect the sheep in his care.

But there's something else here too. When Jesus claimed the title of Good Shepherd, He also applied biblical prophecy to Himself in an unmistakable way:

> The word of the Lord came to me, saying, "Son of man, prophesy against the shepherds of Israel....You eat the fat, you clothe yourselves with the wool, you kill the fatlings, but you do not feed the sheep. The diseased and the weak you have not strengthened, the sick you have not healed, the hurt and crippled you have not bandaged, those gone astray you

have not brought back, the lost you have not sought to find, but with force and hardhearted harshness you have ruled them."…Thus says the Lord God: "Behold I, I Myself, will search for My sheep and will seek them out…I will rescue them…I will bring them…I will feed them…I will cause them to lie down…I will seek that which was lost and bring back that which has strayed and I will bandage the hurt and the crippled and will strengthen the weak and the sick."

—EZEKIEL 34:1, 3-4, 11-16, AMP

We are rightly dismayed when a scandal rocks the Church that involves a Christian in a leadership role. We are disgusted by greed and hypocrisy, particularly by those who claim to be serving God but in fact rewrite Scripture to excuse themselves while lording it over others.

It was no different in the prophet Ezekiel's day, and it was the same in the time of Jesus as well. Men who wore the robes of the priesthood, the leadership of the religious assemblies, lived off those they were supposed to serve. These false shepherds ignored all of their responsibilities.

How can you tell the difference, when false shepherds look good on the surface?

Underscore this fact in your mind: The prophecy reports that God said of Himself: "*I, I Myself, will search for My sheep and seek them out*" (Ezekiel 34:11, AMP). Jesus applied this comparison—the words of God—to Himself. He was so clear that there was no confusion in the mind of His listeners.

How do we know this is so? In the Gospel of John, Jesus' discussion of the Good Shepherd versus the "hirelings" did not occur in isolation. His description of Himself as the Good Shepherd in John 10 is part of a larger discussion.

After Jesus healed the man born blind, the religious leaders, the so-called "shepherds of Israel," immediately hauled the healed man into court and attacked the authority and credibility of Jesus, calling Him a fake and a sinner. They did not rejoice at God's mercy or the miracle that the man had been healed. Envy caused them instead to seek ways to discredit the power and authority of Jesus as the Good Shepherd.

Jesus replies to these accusations:

> I assure you...he who does not enter by the door into the sheepfold, but climbs up some other way is a thief and a robber....The thief comes only in order to steal and kill and to destroy. I came that they might have and enjoy life, and have it in abundance. I am the Good Shepherd.
>
> —JOHN 10:1, 10-11, ESV

Jesus refers to those religious leaders who opposed Him as thieves and, later, as cowardly, hireling shepherds who have no real concern for the flock...the same comparison as made in Ezekiel 34.

Jesus, the Good Shepherd, shows love and mercy to His sheep.

False shepherds seek only to retain their control and power over the lives of others.

THE JUST DUE OF BULLIES

When I was at Shepherds Camp, once a week the son of the *patrone* drove up the mountain to deliver mail and supplies. One week he came with a message for Maria to select two sheep from the herd as his contribution for the annual July 4th picnic.

We all had some apprehension that our own lambs might be selected. They were not the finest of the flock, so would not be missed.

There was one pair of animals we all feared and hated, but they were untouchable. A ewe and her male lamb were pointed out to us as the best examples of physical perfection. He had been personally selected by the *patrone* as part of a future breeding program.

The male was beautiful—bigger by half

than the other lambs his age—but a bully. The first offspring of a large, protective ewe, the pair intimidated the weaker sheep constantly. They were the tyrants of the flock, butting in as others drank, and trampling the best forage, even as they prevented others from grazing.

I and my five ewes and their lambs, sweet-tempered and gentle, were often chased from the water by these two as we tried to approach. Constant correction by Maria and Papa Raul had no effect in altering their aggressive behavior. The mother ewe hissed, growled, and nipped at lambs, and charged at us child shepherds.

That morning, as Maria chatted with the son of the *patrone*, the vicious ewe lunged at my back. Her teeth pinched my arm in a sneak attack. (I still bear that scar over forty years after the encounter.)

As Maria cleaned and dressed the wound on my forearm and wiped my tears, she asked, "Little Bo? The son of *patrone* is here in the pickup. Do you wish to go home?"

I shook my head from side to side. "My lambs need me."

She smiled and kissed me. "You are a good shepherd. Even wounded. Here is good news. The *patrone* has sent word today for us to select two fine sheep for Fourth of July. The sheep who bit you? Her son could have made a fine 4-H lamb. A show lamb at the fair. But you see how they keep the flock stirred up? And he's learning to be mean from his mama. A sneak, a greedy thief, and a bully. Too proud to be content. They band together to steal what belongs to others. The *patrone* will be happy that we send such fine, fat bullies for the picnic."

I could not know it at the time, but the shepherd's response to aggressive behavior of the ewe and her arrogant offspring is reflected in Scripture:

I will bandage the hurt and the crippled and will strengthen the weak and the sick, but I will destroy the hardhearted and perverse; I will feed them with judgment and punishment. As for you, O my flock, thus says the Lord God: Behold I judge between sheep and sheep, between the rams and the great he-goats (the malicious and the tyrants of the pasture).

Is it too little for you that you feed on the best pasture, but must you tread down with your feet the rest of your pasture? And to have drunk of the waters clarified by subsiding, but you must foul the rest of the water with your feet?

—EZEKIEL 34:17-18, AMP

Like Maria, the Lord says He notices the behavior of greedy bullies in His flock, and the Good Shepherd will not stand for arrogance among the strong who achieve their preeminence by tyranny. Scripture gives this warning to those who become strong at the expense of others:

Because you push with side and with shoulder and thrust with your horns all those that have become weak and diseased, till you have scattered them abroad. Therefore will I rescue my flock, and they shall no more be a prey; and I shall judge between sheep and sheep.

—EZEKIEL 34:21-22, AMP

The Good Shepherd will always make multiple attempts to correct and forgive the bad behavior of those sheep in His flock who need an attitude adjustment. But ultimately He is never merciful to evil at the expense of the meek.

Within the hour after I was attacked, the aggressive ewe and her arrogant lamb were on their way down the mountain, where they provided a fine feast at the July 4th, 1959, church picnic.

WHO ARE THE SHEEP?

*Could sheep be...
people like us?*

Know that the Lord, He is God!
It is He Who made us,
and we are His; we are His people,
and the sheep of His pasture.

—Psalm 100:3, ESV

THE SHEEP OF HIS PASTURE

There are three ways in which we are the Lord's flock:

1. He created us. We are His by right of design. He is the patent holder on all Creation.
2. He bought us back from another owner—redeemed us at a terrible price.
3. He provides for us, as long as we let Him. He will not force us to stay in His pasture, but so long as we do, He meets all our needs.

WHAT ABOUT THOSE OUTSIDE THE SHEEPFOLD?

Jesus said in John 10:16, "*I have other sheep that are not of this fold. I must bring and impel those also*" (AMP). This is the point at which the invitation to become part of God's eternal family is enlarged beyond His Chosen People, the Jews, to embrace the rest of humanity. And that means every one of us!

Jesus was confirming the prophecy of Isaiah 42:6: "*I the Lord have called You (the Messiah) for a righteous purpose and in righteousness....I will give You for a covenant to the people (Israel), for a light to the nations (Gentiles)"* (AMP).

And again in Isaiah 49:6: *"I will also give You (the Messiah) for a light to the nations, that My salvation may extend to the end of the earth"* (AMP).

To the *end of the earth!* No one is to be left out—no nation, people, tribe, or tongue is uninvited or unwelcome! This has been the message of the Gospel for 2000 years: *All are welcome to become the sheep of His pasture.*

WHY SUCH AN OFFER?

People often make jokes about sheep: how stupid they are, how smelly, how easily fooled. But God has an alternate view: Sheep are valuable!

Before, during, and since the first-century world of Jesus, many cultures have counted their wealth by their flocks and herds. A family possessing many sheep had access to wool for clothing, milk for cheese, and a ready source of capital that reproduced itself so long as the rains came and the pastures remained and the shepherds were diligent.

What did Jesus say about the man who had a hundred sheep?

> What do you think? If a man has a hundred sheep, and one of them has gone astray and gets lost, will he not leave the ninety-nine on the mountain and go in search of the one that is lost? And if it should be that he finds it, truly I say to you, he rejoices more over it than over the ninety-nine that did not get lost.
>
> —MATTHEW 18:12, AMP

The Bible doesn't compare us to sheep merely because we wander off (which we certainly do, at times), but because we are precious to the Lord. We are worth rescuing! How do we know that's true?

John 3:16 says, "*For God so loved the world that He gave His Only Son, that whoever believes in Him should not perish, but have eternal life*" (ESV). If you were not valuable to God, why would He offer you eternal life? If your life was not precious to Him, why would He sacrifice His Only Son, Jesus, to save you?

WHY IS JESUS
THE BEST SHEPHERD?

*Jesus is not only the Good Shepherd
but the Great Shepherd
and the Chief Shepherd.*

For we do not have a High Priest
(think "Shepherd")
Who is unable to understand and sympathize
and have a shared feeling with our weaknesses
and infirmities and liability to the assaults of temptation,
but One Who has been tempted
in every respect as we are, yet without sinning.

—Hebrews 4:15 (AMP)

A DIVINE MYSTERY

Remember that Jesus—a man, yes, but also the Son of God—was born in a stable? Remember that John the Baptist proclaimed Jesus, *"the Lamb of God, who takes away the sin of the world!"*? (John 1:29).

Jesus is, and will always be, the Shepherd who is also a Sheep. As the Shepherd is the owner of the sheep, He has the authority and the power and the ability to meet their every need. But how does He know what those needs are?

Because He came to earth to live as a man (sheep in this analogy), He knows everything about us and what we face and what we require. The One who can best be your Good Shepherd is the One who lived on earth as a sheep! He experienced weakness, hunger, thirst, deprivation, wounding, betrayal, abandonment…even death. There is nothing—absolutely nothing—you or I can face that Jesus has not already endured and to a greater degree than we will ever have to face.

WHY BOTHER TO BE OUR SHEPHERD?

If we are so lowly and He is so great, why would He stoop to care for us wayward sheep?

Simply this: because He loves us with an implacable love. He created us to love Him...not because He needed our love, but because He IS Love and His love overflowed to us-ward!

Jesus demonstrated that He is the *Good Shepherd* when He laid down His life for His sheep. He died in our place, took our punishment, and satisfied the eternal debt of sin that separated us from God.

Jesus is the *Great Shepherd* because He rose from the dead. It is not enough to die for another. Many good men and women can and have done that. But the Great Shepherd is He who destroys the greatest enemy—death—once and for all. Because of the death and resurrection of Jesus, no one—not Jesus or anyone else—need ever die again. He defeated death and completed our reconciliation with God.

As Hebrews 13:20-21 says, "*May the God of peace, who through the blood of the eternal covenant brought back from the dead our Lord Jesus, that great Shepherd of the sheep, equip you with everything good for doing His will.*"

Finally, Jesus is the *Chief Shepherd*. When He comes again to gather all His sheep to Himself, "*every knee should bow…and every tongue confess that Jesus Christ is Lord*" (Philippians 2:10-11). The staff of our Good Shepherd will be His scepter when we see Him on His throne as King and Lord of all! No matter what false shepherds the wayward sheep of this world have been following, at that moment everyone on earth will acknowledge that Jesus—and only Jesus—is the Chief Shepherd.

This is the same profession of the mystery of faith the Church has proclaimed for 2000 years: "Christ has died. Christ is risen. Christ will come again!"

ME, A SHEPHERD?

*Could sheep
become shepherds?*

Who'll go and help this Shepherd kind,
Help Him the wand'ring ones to find?
Who'll bring the lost ones to the fold,
Where they'll be sheltered from the cold?

—"Bring Them In"
verse 2, words by Alexcenah Thomas

A CALLING BORNE OUT OF LOVE

Jesus of Nazareth is the perfect Good Shepherd because He not only gave His life for us, His sheep, but also because He lived among us as one of us.

Shepherding is a lonely business, and shepherds are grateful for the companionship and aid of worthy sheepdogs. But there are other assistants as well. Within every flock are seasoned rams and ewes—sheep who have trod the valley pastures and mountain trails many times before. Canny, crafty, and attuned to the voice of the shepherd, they act as role models for the flock.

Almost as if the experienced sheep were themselves assistant shepherds.

Those of us who have a little Spanish at our command recognize the connection between the title "Pastor" and the word *shepherd*. Indeed, that is an exact translation.

This is the same challenge to duty Jesus laid on Peter three times: "*If you love Me, feed My sheep*" (John 21:15-17, ESV). Jesus, as the owner of the flock, was appointing Peter an assistant shepherd. Jesus connected Peter's love for Him with responsibility: "Peter, I'm leaving you with a great duty—take care of my sheep."

There may be a temptation to only apply that command to Simon Peter, or the apostles, or to those who bear the title Pastor. But *all* those who love Jesus and are saved by Him are called to be pastors—shepherds, if you will—of the flock of believers. It's our love-borne duty to tend the needs, the hurts, and the education of the lambs and the other sheep. And at times it's a mighty duty, because the sheep don't always behave!

SHEEP...OR SHEPHERD?

When you aren't sure if you want to be called either a sheep or a shepherd, think of the heroic David, the boy shepherd who became the mighty king of Israel and the multi-great-grandfather of the future Messiah. He was not ashamed to proclaim, "*The Lord is MY shepherd*" (Psalm 23:1).

He called himself a sheep, with no sheepishness. But then David himself moved on to become a shepherd of the people of Israel.

A good shepherd is constantly aware of the sheep's needs...even before the sheep know or recognize them. And oftentimes sheep have trouble expressing their needs. They're not sure where it hurts. They become anxious, care-worn, and don't thrive. As a result, they can't produce healthy lambs or good-quality wool.

What are we called to produce? Love in overflowing, world-changing abundance, and baby lambs...new believers in Yeshua Messiah.

We can fulfill neither calling if we are anxious. But we can fulfill both beautifully if we rest in the Good Shepherd's arms, knowing that He will anticipate our needs, provide for us, and move us right where we should be to fulfill our shepherding duties.

SPRING, 1982

It was lambing season. Brock and I and our three small children drove up the narrow mountain road toward our home in Glennville, California. On the left side of the road, a sheep-filled pasture stretched out at the foot of an oak-covered hill. A lone shepherdess stood on a boulder, watching over the flock. Two border collies sat beside her.

I knew at once it was Maria. "Pull over!" I instructed. Rolling down the window, I called to my beloved teacher.

She grinned broadly, leapt from her perch, and beckoned for us all to come see the lambs.

We tumbled out of the car and walked to where ewes and their babies cropped the grass.

Maria seemed unchanged from my childhood memories. She laughed as she hugged me and the kids. Her curly hair seemed a bit more gray, but everything else about her was the same.

"Where's Papa Raul?" I asked.

She looked toward the mountain. "Oh, he's gone home. Last year. You didn't know?"

"No, I hadn't heard. I'm sorry," I replied, thinking she meant Papa Raul had died.

"It's okay. He writes every week," she reassured me. "He got married two months ago to a woman younger than me and says if I come home he has picked out a husband for me, too."

"Are you going?"

"I might like to get married again. Maybe one last summer with my little shepherds? You were the first. Now your kids growing up." She gathered up four-year-old Luke in her arms as if he were a lamb.

I asked, "Who will teach them how to be good shepherds if you leave?"

She kissed my cheek and then each of our children in turn. "You teach them. Just as I taught you and my father taught me, and his father.... And back long before we can remember, the Lord Himself taught the heart of the first shepherd. The line is unbroken. It means something, you know. The Lord Himself is our Shepherd. It really, really means something."

IT'S ALL FOR YOU

*The Good Shepherd deserves
the proper place in your life.
He longs for it.*

Perverse and foolish oft I strayed,
But yet in love He sought me,
And on His shoulder gently laid,
And home, rejoicing, brought me.

—"The King of Love My Shepherd Is"
verse 3, words by Henry W. Baker, 1868

HOW CAN I MAKE JESUS MY GOOD SHEPHERD?

In verse 7 of John 10 Jesus refers to Himself as *"the door of the sheepfold"* (ESV). To become one of His sheep, you must first enter at the right door. As Jesus said, *"I am the Way and the Truth and the Life. No one comes to the Father except through me"* (John 14:6).

It is not enough to know that you need a shepherd.

It is not enough to recognize that Jesus is "a" Good Shepherd.

You must choose Him to be *your* Shepherd by an act of your will. Ask Him to come into your life...cleanse your life...set about healing your wounds.

He won't say no!

Your transformation awaits. All you need is a willing, humble heart to pray this simple prayer:

"Here's my life, Lord Jesus. I surrender it to You. I admit my need for a Savior. By an act of my will I consciously want You to be the Good, Great, and Chief Shepherd of my life...not me."

Why not record this moment when your life changed for all eternity?

———————————————————————————

my signature

———————————————————————————

date

You can be assured that "*If you seek Him, He will be found by you*" (1 Chronicles 28:9)!

WHAT NEXT?

Because you have trusted your life to Jesus, the Redeemer and your Good Shepherd, your sins are forgiven. You are born again, and the Lord promises you have Eternal Life!

You ask, "What do I do now?"

#1 Tell someone.
Tell a Christian friend *right now* that you have asked Jesus to come into your heart. Or e-mail us: brockandbodie@littlebooksofwhy.com.

We'll celebrate with you and pray for you.

> Let us hold unswervingly to the hope we
> profess, for He who promised is faithful.
>
> —HEBREWS 10:23

#2 Read the Bible.
There is only one book you can trust above all others to give you the *truth* about Jesus—the Bible. If any book disagrees with these God-breathed words, it is *not* the truth. Begin by reading the Gospel of John. There are many modern translations that will make the story even more understandable.

> All Scripture is God-breathed and is useful for
> teaching, rebuking, correcting and training in
> righteousness, so that the man of God may be
> thoroughly equipped for every good work.
>
> —2 TIMOTHY 3:16

#3 Find fellowship.

Find a Bible-believing church where you can experience joy, fellowship, and learn about God's Word. Ask
to be baptized (Galatians 3:25-27).

> Let us not give up meeting together...
> but let us encourage one another.
>
> —HEBREWS 10:25

Just as there is no doubt that Jesus, the Good
Shepherd who descended from heaven to sacrifice His
life as the Lamb of God for you, you may be certain
that Jesus is alive and born in your heart *today*!

> Yet to all who received Him, to those who
> believed in His name, He gave the right to
> become children of God—children born not
> of natural descent, nor of human decision...
> but born of God.
>
> —JOHN 1:12-13

ABOUT THE
AUTHORS

For over twenty-five years Bodie and Brock Thoene (pronounced *Tay-nee*) have pursued advanced studies in Jewish history, concentrating on the Jewish roots of Christianity. They are adjunct professors with The Masters College in European history, English literature, and Journalism. They also teach Writing for Publication in association with the University of the Nations, Kona, Hawaii.

Brock holds advanced degrees in History and Education. Besides being an amateur astronomer, he has made the study of biblical Hebrew his life's work. Bodie has degrees in Journalism and Communications. She began her writing career with John Wayne's Batjac Productions.

The Thoenes have written over 45 works of internationally acclaimed historical fiction—including The Zion Chronicles, The Zion Covenant, The Zion Legacy, The Shiloh Legacy, *Shiloh Autumn*, The Galway Chronicles, A.D. Chronicles, and Legends of the West—as well as regular devotional blogs and commentaries. Their weblog can be found at www.thoenebooks.com.

Their novels of pre-World War II Europe (The Zion Covenant series) and the miraculous rebirth of Israel and the Israeli War of Independence (The Zion

Chronicles and The Zion Legacy series) are highly regarded for their historical accuracy, recognized by the American Library Association and Zionist libraries around the world, and widely used in university classrooms to teach history.

That their books have sold more than 10 million copies and have won eight ECPA Gold Medallion awards affirms what millions of readers have already discovered—the Thoenes are not only master stylists but experts at capturing readers' minds and hearts.

Married for over 35 years, the Thoenes have four grown children and six grandchildren. Their assistance to Jews making aliyah to Israel from the countries of the former Soviet Union has been acknowledged by the nation of Israel.

Cofounded by the Thoenes, The Shiloh Light Foundation (www.shilohlightfoundation.org), ships Christian literature and Bibles to prisoners and to members of the U.S. Armed Forces and their families. Through www.familyaudiolibrary.com, the Foundation also produces and provides low-cost Christian audiobooks to those who are visually handicapped and/or learning disabled.

For more information, visit www.thoenebooks.com.

Want to read more about the story of Jesus?

Zion Legacy, by Bodie and Brock Thoene

The Jerusalem Scrolls, The Stones of Jerusalem, and *Jerusalem's Hope*

A mysterious prophet transforms the lives of Miryam of Magdala, Marcus the Centurion, and three Jewish orphans.

A.D. Chronicles® by Bodie and Brock Thoene

First Light
At the darkest time in Jewish history, blind beggar Peniel longs for light…and finds the Healer.

Second Touch
Lily, the leper of the Valley of Mak'ob, discovers that nothing is too hard for God.

Third Watch
The truth about who Jesus is transforms despair into joy for Susanna, Manaen, Zahav, Alexander, and young Hero.

Fourth Dawn
Where is the promised liberator? Signs appear in the heavens, and Mary receives an unusual visitor.

Fifth Seal
Is anywhere far enough from King Herod's evil clutches?

Sixth Covenant
Bethlehem becomes the focus of a terrifying rampage… and the hinge upon which all history turns.

Seventh Day
Stories of miracles abound. Could Yeshua be the long-awaited Messiah?

Discover the Truth through Fiction™